To Mary -
"There's No One Quite Like You"
You've been a good friend
through the years!
Love,
Sue Schott
1996

THERE'S NO ONE QUITE LIKE
YOU

by Sue Schott
illustrated by Rachel Schott

GLOBAL BLOCKS™

10121 Laurel Drive • Eden Prairie, MN 55347-3048

About the Author

SUE SCHOTT is the perfect person to write children's books. She is a mother and grandmother who loves children and loves reading to them. She believes that teaching children how to view themselves in a positive light is critical to their development and self-esteem.

Sue's background is deeply rooted in the values of small midwestern communities. She grew up in Early, Iowa and now lives on a farm in southern Minnesota. As a young girl, it never occurred to her that there was anything a girl could not do if she set her mind to it. In high school she was a cheerleader, yearbook editor, active in the French Club, and even played football with her brother and the neighbor boys on weekends. Sue attended Morningside College in Sioux City, IA and then moved to New York with her husband Lee.

After Sue and her family moved to rural Minnesota, she decided that the school board at her children's school needed a female viewpoint since there had never been a woman on the board. She was elected and served three terms, including 2 years as Chairperson. She made such a contribution that a local organization honored her with a plaque that said, "To Sue Schott, for Outstanding Service to HIS Community." The award had never been given to a woman before. She left the wording as it was and enjoyed the humor of it.

Sue writes the books from the heart. She feels the topics are "as important to children as their vegetables, but reading them should be as much fun as a trip to get ice cream." The other important aspect is that adults enjoy reading her books as much as the children enjoy hearing them read!

The wonderful characters in Sue's books are the creative work of Rachel Schott, Sue's daughter-in-law and mother of Sue's grandchildren. Rachel lives on a farm only two and a half miles from Sue.

Dedication

To my girls, Heather, Stephanie, Rachel and Amara who are all unique and just full of wonderful talent.
(Sue Schott)

For Marty, Britton and Amara. You are the inspiration for all I do. Thank you God!
(Rachel Schott)

© 1995 Sue Schott and Rachel Schott
Printed and bound in the U.S.A.

There's No One Quite Like You   Library of Congress Catalog Card Number: 95-79482   ISBN 1-885374-03-8

Toni was a turtle
with a face so very sad.
Her body and her build, SHE THOUGHT,
were very, very, bad.

"If only I were tall," she mused,
"with legs up to the sky.
I'd be so smart, I'd love myself.
I wouldn't be so shy.

"My shell, it is so dull and broad.
The colors are not right!
If only I were long and lean,
I'd be a pretty sight."

Now down the road lived Geri,

   and she, too, was sad, you see.

She spent her days just dreaming

   as she nibbled on a tree.

"My legs are long, my feet are big

   and I'm so tall and geeky.

I don't like being a giraffe.

   I'm tired of feeling freaky!"

These two young girls were very sad,

so full of deep self-pity.

They felt they were the strangest things

when really, THEY WERE PRETTY!

Pretty on the OUTSIDE

and more lovely on the IN!

But more than that, oh they were smart,

yes, sharper than a pin!

But, oh, they thought too much about

the things that they were not.

They really should have stressed

the good strong qualities they'd got.

she didn't see the turtle

who came from the other way,

singing lovely turtle songs,

her favorite form of play.

Suddenly the two of them surprised, met face to face!

Their chins were sitting on the ground in that peculiar place.

'Cause Geri'd tripped on Toni's shell and then she'd skinned her knee,

fell upon her chin, and hit her head against a tree.

"I heard some pretty singing,"
Geri said EXCITEDLY.
"I think I heard an angel
right before I hit this tree!"

"Oh that was me," said Toni

blushing shyly in reply.

"I'm sorry if I bothered you."

She thought that she would cry!

"Oh, no, I loved it! And I've always wished that I could sing.

With this long throat and vocal chords, I cannot croon a thing!

Your song was inspiration. I relished every note.

If only I could make some music come out of my throat!"

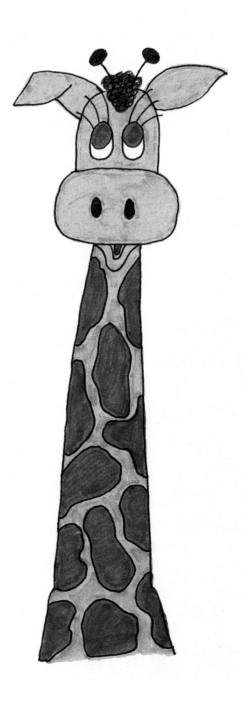

"But," Toni said, "I wish that I

  could count and add like you!

And multiply those numbers

  just the way that big kids do!

If I were tall and smart and lean,

  I'd have just what I want.

I wouldn't even care

  if all my voice could do was grunt!"

"It's clear that I admire you and you admire me,"

    said Geri, as she pulled herself up off the little tree.

"We both have qualities so rare, THERE'S NO ONE QUITE LIKE US!

    We really needn't have a care, we shouldn't have to fuss.

Yes, different makes us special,

    it's what we call unique.

To list our special qualities

    would take almost a week!

If everyone looked just alike and acted just the same,

    then it would be an awful mess each time we played a game!

Our faces all would look the same, no difference, me from you.

    The list would be so very long of things we couldn't do!

We wouldn't have a certain way to talk or laugh or smile.

    Can you imagine life that way? We'd have no special style!

Our colors and our bodies

    and our talents are just fine.

You have the things that you do well

    and I have all of mine.

I think that we are GREAT, the way

that we were meant to be.

And even though it took us running

right into a tree,

we learned there's

NO ONE

QUITE LIKE YOU

and NO ONE

QUITE LIKE ME!"

Look for other products by GLOBAL BLOCKS™

"Everyone Can Be Your Friend"

by Sue Schott, Illustrated by Rachel Schott
ISBN 1-885374-04-6

This book teaches children how to handle anger in a non-violent way. As a bully confronts Geri and Toni, they find a peaceful way to handle him ... and their anger. The two colorful characters use their ingenuity to teach the bully about friendship and make him realize it is more fun to play with others than it is to fight. The rhymes and the bright colors will delight children and adults while teaching gentleness at the same time. **$11.95**, plus $1.80 s&h.

Flip*It™ in Spanish
ISBN 1-885374-02-X
Flip*It™ in French
ISBN 1-885374-01-1
Flip*It™ in English
ISBN 1-885374-00-3

Children have fun flipping the top half and bottom half of the pages to match over-sized numbers with vividly colored pictures. Learn colors and numbers in French, Spanish and English. Books designed by teachers for children 3 - 8. **$4.95 each** or $12.00 for all 3 Flip*It books, plus $1.80 s&h.

Geri and Toni Growth Chart

Have fun growing with Geri and Toni. Full-color chart measures to 57" tall. Spaces to insert pictures of your growing child.
$4.95, plus $1.80 s&h.

Global Blocks™ - 30 hardwood blocks - in bright non-toxic colors.
· In Spanish, French, or German.
· Learn a foreign alphabet.
· Learn 60 foreign words.
· Learn numbers 1 - 10, colors and shapes.
· Puzzle map shows continents and oceans.
· Be creative through manipulation of shapes.

$34.95, plus $4.50 shipping charge.

Parents' Choice Award Winner!

If your local bookseller or toy store does not have these items in stock, they can order them for you. You may order them directly from Global Blocks, Inc. for the listed price of each item, plus shipping and handling (s&h) for each item, but try your bookstore or toy store first.

Heaven Sent Creations
RR 2 Box 136
New Sweden, MN 56074
(507)246-5240

"Educational Toys and Books"